YOUR KNOWLEDGE HAS VALUE

- We will publish your bachelor's and master's thesis, essays and papers

- Your own eBook and book - sold worldwide in all relevant shops

- Earn money with each sale

Upload your text at www.GRIN.com and publish for free

Bibliographic information published by the German National Library:

The German National Library lists this publication in the National Bibliography; detailed bibliographic data are available on the Internet at http://dnb.dnb.de .

This book is copyright material and must not be copied, reproduced, transferred, distributed, leased, licensed or publicly performed or used in any way except as specifically permitted in writing by the publishers, as allowed under the terms and conditions under which it was purchased or as strictly permitted by applicable copyright law. Any unauthorized distribution or use of this text may be a direct infringement of the author s and publisher s rights and those responsible may be liable in law accordingly.

Imprint:

Copyright © 2016 GRIN Verlag, Open Publishing GmbH
Print and binding: Books on Demand GmbH, Norderstedt Germany
ISBN: 9783668237995

This book at GRIN:

http://www.grin.com/en/e-book/324070/treatments-for-borderline-personality-disorder-bpd-an-overview-over

Danielle LaBeau

**Treatments For Borderline Personality Disorder (BPD).
An Overview over Existing Research**

GRIN Publishing

GRIN - Your knowledge has value

Since its foundation in 1998, GRIN has specialized in publishing academic texts by students, college teachers and other academics as e-book and printed book. The website www.grin.com is an ideal platform for presenting term papers, final papers, scientific essays, dissertations and specialist books.

Visit us on the internet:

http://www.grin.com/

http://www.facebook.com/grincom

http://www.twitter.com/grin_com

Borderline Personality Disorder (BPD) is a complicated psychological disorder that is more common than many believe. This personality disorder involves irregular emotion and behavior and a severe lack in mental awareness/reasoning. Because of the vast and acute criteria it takes to be diagnosed as a person with BPD, these patients are looked on to be some of the most difficult patients to treat. To date, there is no medication that has been assigned to BPD. For this reason, many clinicians turn away patients with BPD because they are unskilled in their knowledge in how to treat BPD and because of the grueling time and commitment it takes. Not only are clinicians hesitant to take on a patient with BPD, the patient is often unwilling to stick with the process of management of their personality disorder for numerous reasons (O'connell & Dowling, 2014).

It is thought that persons with BPD suffered with emotional vulnerability at very young ages, which lead to powerful emotional anguish and pain in their adult years. This pain and distress is often followed by passionate and uncontrollable anger, manipulation, and a desire for attention (O'Connell & Dowling, 2014).

BDP can be classified mainly as psychosocial instability in many different faucets. Psychosocial instability takes its form in the inability to maintain friendships and relationships. Although there is a desire to be loved and accepted, most times these people reject others because of their fear of being rejected. In the same way, may people who are in relationships, be it friends, family, or significant others, cannot take the burden of dealing with a person suffering from such a complicated personality disorder. Not only are personal relationships hard to maintain, jobs are also hard for a person with BPD to maintain. Because of this, poverty is prevalent among those who suffer with

BPD. All of these factors lead to identity issues that can lead to the abuse of drugs and/or alcohol and eating disorders. Because of the deep emotional pain that is present, most of the times BPD patients struggle with self-harm, eventually leading to suicide. It is safe to say all aspects these people's lives are at a high risk for being completely instable (Jorgensen et al., 2013).

One crucial part of being a person who has BPD is that there is a high level of fear of being abandoned or alone in life. If there is an interpersonal relationship, it is usually very intense (Levy et al., 2006). This is another reason that clinicians are weary of treating a person with BPD. The patient might become overly attached to the clinician and the clinician might unintentionally let his or her patient down, causing even more emotional pain and distress. So many factors come into play when it comes to setting a plan to treat someone with BPD, which is why there is no set model, only theories that are still being tested.

Cognitive Behavioral Therapy (CBT) is one that is widely used among clinicians to treat many and most psychological disorders and even can help just to problem solve. CBT is used to help a patient identify his or her problem(s), identify and change thinking that should ultimately lead to changed behavior and finally changed emotional responses. Another primary focus of CBT is to help change the beliefs of his or herself and of others. This type of therapy must take place with a high level of cooperation from the patient and the clinician.

Some researchers of BPD came up with the idea that the most immediate cause for treatment for those with BPD was the suicide rates and harmful drastic accidents due to such instable behavior. In a research article by Davidson, K., Norrie, J., Tyrer, P.,

Gumley, A., Tata, P., Murray, H., & Palmer, S (2006), patients between the ages of 18-65 were used in a study to determine the if emergency related accidents, hospitalization for psychiatrics, and suicidal acts would be lessened by the use of CBT combined with treatment as usual (TAU) and just TAU on people who fit the qualifications of BPD. TAU involved in and outpatient programs, nurses and other clinical services to treat the patients. Another outcome that was looked for that was considered secondary was to see id self-harm acts and behaviors not caused by accidents were lessened.

Interestingly, the primary outcome showed no significant differences in using CBT combined with TAU and just TAU. There was, however, a great reduction in suicidal acts by the method of CBT combined with TAU. The secondary outcome of the study only showed that there were only some significant differences between CBT combined with TAU and just TAU. Although this study was not able to show drastic differences, since the time of this study there have been more to prove that CBT does in fact reduce anxiety and suicidal behavior. Because this particular study was unable to prove much, it was determined that more research needs to be done how treatments may be most effective (Davidson et al., 2006).

CBT can take place in many forms. In addition, there can be branches of CBT. One of the branches is Dialectical Behavior Therapy (DBT). The use of dialectics is the show that there are to different points of view that may be opposing at hand at all times. The process that DBT uses is to bring the two opposing points of view together and make the patient aware of these two opposing views and some how combine them. This helps a person by realizing that there is more emotions and thoughts involves than just his or her own. The reason that a person with BPD may have a problem doing this on his or her own is because they are emotionally vulnerable and have been at one point in his or her life or another combined with a living environment that declined to acknowledge these emotions. The key to DBT is emotional validation (Harned, Banawan, & Lynch, 2006).

One of the main focuses of DBT is using mindfulness. Mindfulness is a skill used to teach people to experience his or her thoughts, emotions, or environment without judging one way or another. This skill can help a person with BPD become more accepting of not only his or herself, but of their surroundings. This can reduce anxiety levels as well as reaction time. Best of all, it validates his or her emotions.

The part of DBT that is similar to CBT is that DBT uses opposite action. Opposite action is the combination of behavioral exposure and cognitive modification. The way these work together is by making the patient aware when an emotion is present and instead of acting on that emotion, use an opposite action to that emotion. The end result of this type of skill is to change the behavior and the emotion, just like what the crux of CBT teaches.

In a study conducted by O'Connell, B., & Dowling, M. (2014), DBT was used to teach new skills to those with BPD. The purpose of the study was to focus on five of the personality traits of those with BPD, openness to experience, agreeableness, conscientiousness, extraversion, and neuroticism. Two groups of people with BPD were chosen. The first group was patients with BPD who just began their 8-week DBT model, and the second group was those who had already finished the model in the past three years. All the participants who were involved were to fill out a questionnaire about the five focused personality traits. The study resulted in showing that those who already did the 8-week DBT model scored lower in neuroticism and higher in consciousness than those who had not completed the model. Since there were no other significant changes, it was again determined that there needed to be further studies done to find a treatment or to even prove the effectiveness of DBT for those who suffer with BPD.

Another branch off of CBT is a form of therapy known as Schema Focused Therapy (SFT). It is a combination of CBT, the use and knowledge of attachment theory, and it uses Gestalt's techniques. SFT may prove to work well because it uses the knowledge of attachment theory unlike the CBT and one of its branches, DBT. As explained before, those who sufferer with BPD are likely to be unable to sustain relationships and jobs because they feel a strong sense of loneliness, fear of abandonment and lack of stability in themselves. Attachment problems are thought to have started at a young age of a person who now suffers with BPD. The Gestalt technique that is used in SFT comes into play here by then having the patient confront emotional damages of the past (Nadort et al., 2009).

Although studies in the past have shown that SFT resulted in fewer acts of self harm, suicides, and an improvement in personality, a study done by Nadort, M., Arntz, A., Smit, J. H., Giesen-Bloo, J., Eikelenboom, M., Spinhoven, P., van Dyck, R. (2009) wanted to study the effectiveness of SFT further by adding a crisis support group that worked longer and extra hours to be readily available whenever a patient needed help. This particular study was done with 60 participants between the ages of 18-60 years of age and 30 therapists. Therapy was held for 45 minutes twice every day for each patient. It lasted 18 months and data was collected at the 6 month, 12 month, and 18 month mark and then once three years after the study was final. The change in each patient was recorded in ranges of behavioral and cognitive techniques within the therapist-patient relationship and with outside activities, relationships, and the emotional recovery of past traumas. The study showed to be effective, however the evidence was not motivating enough to keep therapists on call after regular hours (Nadort et al., 2009).

CBT can be used for any person for whatever the need for therapy is. However, DBT and SFT were specifically created for patients with BPD. What can be concluded is that CBT alone is not enough to help patients who suffer with BPD. Since then, the development of DBT and SFT have added elements specific to treating BPD but were still insufficient in showing that those forms of treatments were capable of being the go-to form of therapy for those who suffer with BPD. The net section of this paper moves on from CBT and forms of CBT and focuses on psychotherapy.

Mentalization Based Therapy (MBT) is a form of psychotherapy. The main idea behind this therapy is to separate the patient from thoughts and feelings and to consider the views of others and how their view might be accepted although there is a difference in opinions. This may sound similar to what CBT is. However, they are two different things.

> "In mentalization-based therapy (MBT), the concept of mentalization is emphasized, reinforced and practiced within a safe and supportive psychotherapy setting. Because the approach is psychodynamic, therapy tends to be less directive than cognitive-behavioral approaches, such as dialectical behavior therapy(DBT), another common treatment approach for borderline personality disorder (Grohol & read, n.d.)."

MBT also focuses on working on interpersonal behaviors by going through events and emotions that had occurred in the past of a patient's life (Jorgensen et al., 2013).

In a study conducted by, Jorgensen, C. R., Freund, C., Boye, R., Jordet, H., Andersen, D., & Kjolbye, M. (2013), MBT was tested by randomly dividing 111 patients with BPD into either supportive group therapy or MBT. MBT was held weekly for 45 minutes while supportive group therapy lasted 1 ½ hours weekly. All patients also participated in psycho-educational programs once a month for six months. Giving the patients a survey to fill out every three months tested the methodology. Unfortunately, some patients refused fill out these surveys, which resulted in a loss of data. One of the scales that were used to test the results was a Global Assessment Functioning Scale (GAF). The GAF showed that MBT worked better than supportive group therapy. However, the other ways to test the results showed that both MBT and supportive group therapy were just as helpful for patients with BPD.

Another form of psychotherapy that is used in treatment of BPD is transference-focused therapy (TFT). MBT is similar to TFT both use mentalization and are both psychotherapies that focus on the factors that caused the attachment issues and how they play out into manipulation, self-defense, differing ones thoughts from another's, fears of being abandoned or alone. On the other hand, TFT is also similar to SFT because of the great focus on attachment theory. TFT specifically works, however by focusing on containing harmful acted out behaviors though clarification confrontation and identifying the interpersonal and relational patterns. The therapist focuses on helping by building the relationship between the clinicians and patients so that they can then apply insights they learn into other situations outside of therapy.

A study conducted by Levy, K. N., Meehan, K. B., Kelly, K. M., Reynoso, J. S., Weber, M., Clarkin, J. F., & Kernberg, O. F. (2006) made its primary goal to assess the attachment levels in those who suffer from BPD. 90 participants between the ages of 18-50 years old were randomly assigned to TFT, DBT or SPT (supportive psychotherapy) for a year.

The Adult Attachment Interview (AAI) assessed the level of attachment each patient identified with. The AAI placed each patient in one of five categories: secure/autonomous (F), dismissing (D), enmeshed/preoccupied (E), unresolved/declassified (U/D), and cannot classify (CC). A secure/autonomous person is well organized and classifies his or her relationships as influential and valuable. Those who dismiss do not value relationships and even have a rough time recalling events from their past. Enmeshed/Preoccupied individuals often refer to their parents as being overbearing and guilt inducing. As adults these people will even continue to try to please parents out of passive aggressive behavior. These types of people also have a hard time putting sentences together to explain past and present relationships (Levy et al., 2006).

In addition to the attachment assessment, the reflective functioning (RF) coding scale was used to assess cognition on a scale that ranges from 1-9. A 1 on the RF scale meant that there was little to no mentalization and a 9 meant that there was concrete reasoning (Levy et al., 2006).

After the 12-month period, patients showed a significant change in attachment levels for the better in TFT, but not in the other two treatments. Significant changes were also seen as a result of TFT with the patients' ability to function better and be more cognitively aware by their ratings following treatment on the RF scale. Little change was shown on the RF scale for the other two treatments (Levy et al., 2006).

It can be concluded from the two studies done using psychotherapy that the results were more concrete than those of CBT or branches of CBT. However, no study used the same tools to arrive at their conclusions, therefore resulting into a need for further, more accurate studies. The only study that used several different forms of therapy specific to BPD was the study on TFT.

Developments seem to have been made over time since the invention of CBT being used to treat BPD throughout with the greatest focus being on attachment theory. Several of the articles that study the attachment theory believe that attachment issues stem from the childhood of such patients. For this reason, it can also be deduced that BPD is a learned personality disorder. If this is true, advancements in using attachment theory in treatments would be most helpful because attachment theory focuses on getting to the root of the problem. In theory, clinicians can be used to help the client identify the root of the problem and start restructuring the mind from there. This being said, there has been an expansion in treatment for BPD that focuses on the control and regulation of emotion.

The S.T.E.P.P.S. (Systems Training for Emotional Predictability and Problem Solving) program was developed to bring awareness and management skills of thoughts, feelings, and actions or behaviors. STEPPS helps enforce goal setting, a healthy lifestyle, leisure, health monitoring, and avoiding self-harm. The out-patient program usually lasts 20 weeks and is taught by a manual. STEPPS was the first program of its kind to use psychoeducation and group support for BPD (Black et al., 2009).

A study done by Black, D. W., Allen, J., St. John, D., Pfohl, B., McCormick, B., & Blum, N. (2009 selected participants for the study if they were 18 years or older and were not be diagnosed with any other disorder, substance abuse, or have attended a STEPPS program before. The results show that attending a minimum of 15 STEPPS sessions brought about the most improvement among those suffering with BPD and that with 15 or more sessions, the improvement of BPD was much greater than those who attended less than 15 STEPPS sessions. However, because so many participants dropped out, data was limited.

Finally, evidence from the past has shown that Omega -3 fatty acids improved other mood disorders. Omega-3 fatty acids include eicosapentaenoic acid and docosahexaenoic acid, which is most commonly found in seafood. Since there have been no medications developed for BPD, Omega-3 fatty acids were thought to be a healthy alternative.

Zanarini, M. C., & Frankenburg, F. R. (2003) conducted a study with 20 subjects with BPD were either randomly assigned to Omega-3 fatty acids or a placebo for two months. During the two months, each subject was seen every week for the first month and every other week for the second month. The results of these meetings were measured on two scales: the Modified Overt Aggression Scale and the Montgomery-Asberg Depression rating Scale. All subjects who took the Omega 3- fatty acids showed great reduction in depression and aggression than those who took the placebo. The limitations to the study were that depression and aggression were the only attributes studied and the study was only tested on women.

To conclude, although many treatments to this day are being carried out to treat those who suffer from BPD, it is clear that there is a need for more studies on each treatment to develop more concrete evidence. Although results from CBT and its branches' studies show less significant results than that of two psychotherapies, it cannot be ruled out that forms of CBT are not as useful. The reason behind this is because the measurement methods were not the same across all studies. Also, it can be noted that at least one theory that is continuing to hold fast and develop for the treatment of BPD and that is attachment theory. Knowledge and treatment are becoming more prevalent to this day which is why there are now even natural supplements for those with BPD and even a psychoeducational program. If research continues, there will be increasingly more effective forms of treatment, knowledge, and proper diagnosis of BPD.

References:

Grohol, J. M., & read, P. D. ~ 1 min. (n.d.). Mentalization Based Therapy (MBT). Retrieved March 4, 2016, from http://psychcentral.com/lib/mentalization-based-t herapy-mbt/

Levy, K. N., Meehan, K. B., Kelly, K. M., Reynoso, J. S., Weber, M., Clarkin, J. F., & Kernberg, O. F. (2006). Change in attachment patterns and reflective function in a randomized control trial of transference-focused psychotherapy for borderline personality disorder. *Journal of Consulting and Clinical Psychology*, 74(6), 1027– 1040. http://doi.org/10.1037/0022-006X.74.6.1027

Dialectical Behavior Therapy (DBT) in the Treatment of Borderline Personality Disorder. *Journal of Psychiatric & Mental Health Nursing*, 21(6), 518–525. http://doi.org/10.1111/jpm.12116

Davidson, K., Norrie, J., Tyrer, P., Gumley, A., Tata, P., Murray, H., & Palmer, S. (2006). The Effectiveness of Cognitive Behavior Therapy for Borderline Personality Disorder: Results From the Borderline Personality Disorder Study of Cognitive Therapy (boscot) Trial. *Journal of Personality Disorders*, 20(5), 450– 465. http://doi.org/10.1521/pedi.2006.20.5.450

Jørgensen, C. R., Freund, C., Bøye, R., Jordet, H., Andersen, D., & Kjølbye, M. (2013). Outcome of Mentalization-Based and Supportive Psychotherapy in Patients with Borderline Personality Disorder: a Randomized Trial. *Acta Psychiatrica Scandinavica*, 127(4), 305–317. http://doi.org/10.1111/j.1600-0447.2012.01923.x

Nadort, M., Arntz, A., Smit, J. H., Giesen-Bloo, J., Eikelenboom, M., Spinhoven, P., … v an Dyck, R. (2009). Implementation of Outpatient Schema Therapy for

Borderline Personality Disorder: Study Design. *BMC Psychiatry, 9,* 64. http://doi.org/http://dx.doi.org.hodges.idm.oclc.org/10.1186/1471-244X-9-64

Black, D. W., Allen, J., St. John, D., Pfohl, B., McCormick, B., & Blum, N. (2009). Predictors of Response to Systems Training for Emotional Predictability and Problem Solving (STEPPS) for Borderline Personality Disorder: An Exploratory Study. *Acta Psychiatrica Scandinavica, 120*(1), 53–61. http://doi.org/10.1111/j.1600-0447.2008.01340.x

Zanarini, M. C., & Frankenburg, F. R. (2003). Omega-3 fatty Acid Treatment of Women with Borderline Personality Disorder: A Double-Blind, Placebo-Controlled Pilot Study. *The American Journal of Psychiatry, 160*(1), 167–9.

YOUR KNOWLEDGE HAS VALUE

- We will publish your bachelor's and master's thesis, essays and papers

- Your own eBook and book - sold worldwide in all relevant shops

- Earn money with each sale

Upload your text at www.GRIN.com
and publish for free